THE INDIAN TEXANS

The Indian Texans
Authors: Thomas H. Guderjan and Carol S. Canty

©1989: The University of Texas
Institute of Texan Cultures at San Antonio

Rex H. Ball, Executive Director

International Standard Book Number 0-86701-038-X

First edition, second printing, 1994

This publication was made possible, in part, by grants from Dorothy and James T. Doyle and the Houston Endowment, Inc.

Printed in the United States of America

Cover: *Fights-with-a-Feather, a Waco chief, by George Catlin*
Back cover: *Trinidad Granillo, cacique of the Tigua Indians from 1982 until his death, photographed by Bill Wright, Abilene*

Library of Congress Cataloging-in-Publication Data
Guderjan, Thomas H.
    The Indian Texans / Thomas H. Guderjan and Carol S. Canty.
      p. cm. — (The Texians and the Texans)
    Bibliography: p.
    Includes index.
    ISBN 0-86701-038-X
    1. Indians of North America—Texas—History. I. Canty, Carol S., 1935-
II. Title. III. Series.
E78.T4G83 1989
976.4'00497—dc20   89-4893
                                                                               CIP

THE INDIAN TEXANS

A Comanche family

The earliest recorded contact in Texas between native Americans and Europeans occurred in 1528 when a small party of Spaniards led by Álvar Núñez Cabeza de Vaca landed on the coast in what may have been Karankawa territory. This brief encounter between two small groups of people was the first step toward profound change. Slowly the people who lived in the vast region would be displaced by the foreigners. However, for at least another 200 years after the first meeting, the land continued to be easily controlled by the Indians. Tribes fought over territory or formed alliances for mutual protection. New groups moved into the area, while others were pushed out. The ebb and flow of power was between native populations, not between Indians and Europeans.

Early contacts between Indians and Europeans were erratic—sometimes friendly and sometimes hostile. It was often with the help of Indians that Spaniards were able to survive in this strange land. The natives were secure in their environment and generally tolerant of the newcomers. However, as Spaniards established settlements and gained power, they wanted to reshape Indian culture in the European mold, but profound cultural and language differences were greater barriers to understanding than the ocean which had separated the Europeans from the Indians.

The Spaniards, Frenchmen, and later European immigrants in what is now Texas were members of complex cultures whose societies were composed of large heterogeneous populations bound together through formal institutions of government and written laws. The people were from various backgrounds and specialized in many occupations: they were teachers, farmers, merchants, shopkeepers, priests, soldiers, lawyers, and so on. Members of society depended on each other for mutual support and shared technology. Goods and services were paid for either with money or through exchange of goods. Individual ownership of land was every man's dream.

Ownership and control of land reflected the European's view of himself as separate from nature and the supernatural. Man sought to dominate nature, and had learned through technology and science to manage many resources, including agriculture and metalworking. On the other hand, while man could

3

control nature to some extent, he was at the mercy of God, creator and director of the universe. Men appealed to God through prayer for help, and if human beings sinned against Him, they asked for forgiveness and promised repentance.

Native American societies were small, isolated, homogeneous groups, usually without the kinds of formal government, education, or religion needed to structure large populations. Kinship was the organizing principle of Indian society. People were related through blood and marriage or by non-kin groupings which bound them to one another with strong bonds. Families were self-sufficient, and there were few specialists, with the exception of shamans, or medicine men. Each man was soldier-hunter-lawyer-trader, and each woman was cultivator-seamstress-craftswoman-manufacturer. Members of society were bound together by shared traditions. They shared feelings of what was right and wrong, and what was the good life. Decisions and action on war, hunting, planting and harvesting, education of young, and good fortune or bad were shared by all. Shared distribution of resources was the economic base of the society. Land was used by all. The idea that an individual could own a piece of earth was inconceivable.

Man, nature, and the supernatural were not separate but each part of a whole, whose balance had to be maintained through care and respect. While most groups believed in a supreme being, they also believed that supernatural power surrounded them in various forms. The native American perceived souls in all natural things—in animals, plants, and objects such as certain rocks or places. Through prayer, man could ask spirits, particularly spirits of animals, to share their power or to bring good fortune. These religious beliefs were labeled superstition by Europeans, who could no more understand them than they could comprehend many other Indian cultural traditions.

Adding to the confusion on the part of the Spaniards, the natives of the region belonged to many distinct groups with different languages and cultural variations. Several linguistic families were represented among Texas Indians, indicating emigrations from many areas of North America. The immigrants learned to adapt to the diverse geography of Texas and to use the natural resources particular to each area. Therefore, the Texas of the Indian was as much a setting for diverse lifestyles and economies as it is today for ranching, agriculture, oil, and service economies.

Although Indian peoples hunted animals and gathered plants for food, there were four major subsistence patterns among the indigenous societies. People in the rugged, sparse environment of the coastal areas depended on fish and vegetable products they gathered for subsistence. In far southwest Texas along the Rio Grande lived groups of horticulturists who planted crops and tilled the soil with simple tools, and depended on rainfall and natural soil moisture for sufficient water. The rich land of East Texas supported several societies based on horticulture, who often utilized fields for two crops in the same year. They raised a variety of vegetables—corn, squash, beans, and tobacco. An 18th century innovation in the Texas region was the horse-mounted societies, which utilized buffalo as their major source of food. After Spaniards introduced the horse to the North American continent in the 16th century, groups of Indians adopted the animal and moved into the plains of northwest and central Texas. Indians who utilized each of these subsistence bases had many cultural traits which were unique to each society, and each was as different from the other as the Spanish were from the French or the English.

WHO WERE THE FIRST "TEXANS"?

The first Australopithicines, man's predecessors, lived in Africa by 3.5 million years ago. By 1.8 million years ago, *Homo habilis,* the first humans, lived in the same area. And by 40,000 years ago, *Homo sapiens,* fully modern people, were living in Europe and the Near East. From there people spread throughout the world. When did they arrive in America? This has become one of the greatest mysteries of the archaeology of the New World, the unknown world brought to the eyes of Europeans by Columbus and other explorers of his time.

It is a mystery with as many answers as there are archaeologists asking the question. Many archaeological sites have been believed to be very old, as old as 100,000 years. Today, though, none of these very

The first Americans cross the Bering Strait following herds of large game across the tundra.

old dates have been widely accepted. There always seems to be something wrong in each case, which casts the shadow of doubt or the specter of fraud on the findings.

PALEO-INDIANS

It is clear, though, that by about 12,000 years ago, people lived all over North and South America. These people, whom we call the "Paleo-Indians," or "Old Indians," lived when the last of the most recent glaciers were retreating. The climate was cooler and wetter. Where we now find arid high plains, there were ponds and trees. Although it is hard to imagine a place called "Lubbock Lake" today, it is the appropriate name for a Paleo-Indian site near Lubbock, Texas. Aside from the climate, the animals which lived at the time were different from today's. Horses, sloths, mammoths, mastodons, and a large type of buffalo all were found at the time but died out by 10,000 years ago.

They were one of the major sources of food for the Paleo-Indians. At sites like Blackwater Draw, New Mexico, Naco and Lehner in southern Arizona, and many others on the southern high plains in Colo-

Artist's rendering of "Midland Minnie," a woman who lived 9,000 years ago near Midland, Texas

Paleo-Indians and later people used the "jump-kill technique" of stampeding bison over cliffs and into arroyos.

rado and Texas, these extinct animals were found to have been killed and butchered by Paleo-Indians. Archaeologists believed that the Paleo-Indians followed herds of these animals, living entirely on the bounty of the hunt. At Bonfire Shelter near Langtry, Texas, a "jump-kill" site was found. Paleo-Indians had chased buffalo over a cliff to their deaths. This technique yielded a tremendous amount of meat and hides.

Archaeologists once thought that the extinct, big-game animals were the only source of food. New information from Lubbock Lake and other sites, however, made them change their point of view. At Lubbock Lake, Paleo-Indians had killed small game and collected wild grasses and other plants to round out their diet. This means that in addition to chasing herds of animals, Paleo-Indians knew their territories well enough that they would regularly return to collect seasonal plant foods and kill the small game which came to the ancient ponds on the plains to feed and drink.

Paleo-Indians seem to have lived in small, family-oriented bands. Perhaps there were never more than 20 or so people in each band. Intermarriage among these bands probably kept their numbers stable. When a band became too large to move about easily, a new "splinter" band was formed. These people did not use cloth or pottery, and no North American Indians ever used much metal. They made their tools from stone and wood and the bones of the animals they hunted. Their shelters and clothes were made of hide. Everything that the group used had to be made from the resources available in the environment in which they lived.

THE ARCHAIC PEOPLE

By about 8,000 years ago the glaciers had melted, and the climate of the world had shifted more or less to what it is today. The big-game animals of the plains had also become extinct. Only the American buffalo, *Bison bison*, remained as the great animal of the plains. The numbers of people had vastly increased from the Paleo-Indian times.

They lived differently, as well. They were hunters and gatherers like their ancestors, but they did not travel as far, and they lived in bigger groups. In a sense, they had begun to "settle in." Archaeologists find that these Archaic people made a much wider variety of specialized tools than the Paleo-Indians. Very large deposits of the remains of daily life have been found, indicating that people lived in single locations longer, perhaps never leaving except for hunting and collecting trips. There are more and bigger archaeological sites from this time than before. Near the end of the Archaic times, in a number of places in Texas, the remains of buildings and evidence of permanent settlement exist. Near San Marcos, Corpus Christi, El Paso, and in East Texas as well, Archaic structures have led archaeologists to conclude that these people lived in the same place all year.

In the Trans-Pecos area of Texas, some of the most important evidence of Archaic culture in America is found. The Trans-Pecos, that area where the Pecos River joins the Rio Grande, is a dry, seemingly desolate place. Deep canyons dissect those flat desert lands. In these canyons are rockshelters carved by flowing water ages ago. Not surprisingly, the ancient people of the Trans-Pecos used these shelters as campsites. They are shaded and cool when the summer sun beats down on the desert, and they give protection from rain and snow.

They are also extremely dry, so that very little rots. Woven mats, sandals, nets, and food remains are almost as intact today as they were thousands of years ago. Archaeologists talk of the "perfect preservation" of materials in these shelters. Even human feces, or coprolites, remain from these ancient inhabitants. Because of this situation, equaled only in the highest of the Andean mountains in South America, archaeologists have learned much about how these people lived. It is also because of this dryness that their art has survived.

The Archaic people of the Trans-Pecos area in Texas are world renowned for the spectacular rock art tradition which can be seen today. Not just the mere doodles of children, the rock art of the Pecos area is part of the culture that produced it. Figures of shamans, or medicine men, tower 16 feet above the ground. To paint some of these figures, scaffolding would have to have been built. We may never know the full and true meaning of this art; we do know that artists, thousands of years dead, have left us with their work to ponder.

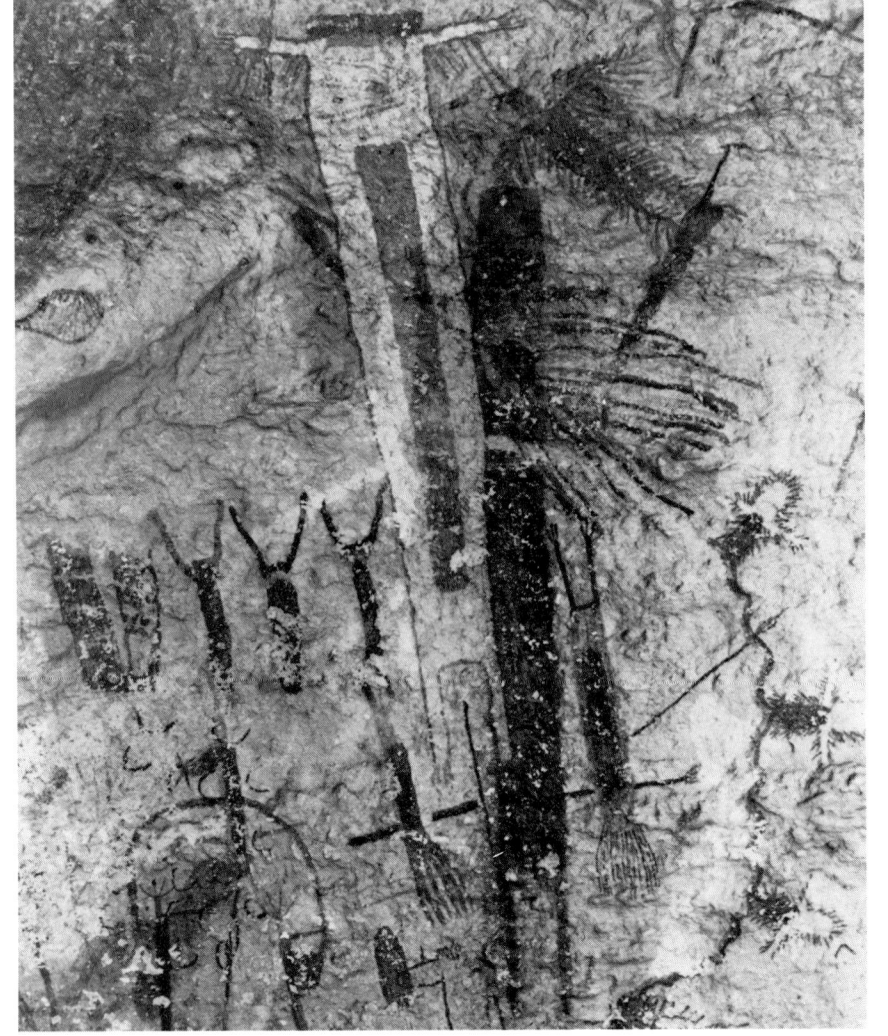

AGRICULTURE AND THE NEO-INDIANS

While rock artists painted the sides of cliffs in Texas, people in central Mexico were experimenting with plants. The discovery of the agricultural triumvirate of corn, beans, and squash was to become the most profoundly revolutionary event in the Americas before Columbus.

The "White Shaman," an Archaic-period pictograph from the Lower Pecos River area

Beans of many kinds were cultivated in North America. Beans contain a tremendous amount of protein, needed in a diet which is low in meat. Unfortunately, this protein is not in a form that humans can easily absorb. Corn, originally a wild Mexican grass, contains an amino acid which breaks down the protein in beans so that people can use it efficiently. Finally, squashes, such as pumpkins and gourds, add trace minerals and other needed dietary elements. A well-balanced meal can be obtained from a corn tortilla with beans and squash on the side.

By shortly after the time of Christ, the technology to grow corn reached North America. It became the "staff of life" for many Indian societies. Large numbers of people could live in one place, permanently. In fact, they had to. No longer could a group of people pack up and move their homes miles away. By adopting agriculture, people had to adapt to agriculture as well. Fields had to be tended, protected against animals and other people alike. Communities grew, rather than splintering off into small groups.

In Texas several groups of people adopted this new way of life. We call those people who adopted a settled, agricultural way of life "Neo-Indians." In East Texas the Caddos and Wichitas became farmers in the broad river bottoms. In far southwest Texas the people whom archaeologists call the "Mogollon" farmed the narrow strip of fertile land along the Rio Grande and at La Junta, where the Rio Grande joins the Rio Conchos. They also grew corn in the sand dunes of the Hueco Bolson, the large flat basin between the Franklin and Hueco mountains near El Paso.

Mysteries abound in the archaeology of Texas. When did the first people come to Texas? What is the meaning of the rock art of the Pecos area? Along the Canadian River, running from New Mexico to Oklahoma through the Texas Panhandle, the remains of stone-walled villages still can be found. However, when the first Europeans searched for the mythical city of Quivera in the area, no farming communities existed in the Panhandle of Texas—the region was the domain of the Apaches. Today we know that these villages were built during the 12th and 13th centuries A.D. Whoever built them seem to have moved into the area from elsewhere . . . but where? They brought new tools, new architecture, new kinds of pottery, and they were farmers. Where did they go? There is no evidence of battles or of disease, but they were gone when the Spanish arrived. Archaeologists call them the Antelope Creek Focus people, after the location of one of their villages. We do not know what they called themselves or what *any* group of people called themselves before the Europeans arrived. So, we use our names for them.

Archaeologists excavate an ancient Antelope Creek Focus village in the Panhandle of Texas.

ARRIVAL OF EUROPEANS

Spaniards, Frenchmen, and Anglo-Americans exploited the land and its inhabitants in different ways. Consequently, their attitudes towards the Indians were often different. The people of New Spain (now Mexico) wanted to make subjects of the Indians, although as a servant class. The French wanted to establish a trading empire in the New World. Later, Anglo-Americans wanted to disregard the Indians completely and settle the country for themselves. The United States did not grant citizenship to Indians until the 20th century.

Spain claimed Texas but did little to colonize it until after 1684, when Frenchmen began to settle in the eastern region. However, French influence was short-lived and confined to the eastern and northern frontiers. Most Frenchmen came as traders and businessmen, not as official representatives of government. They were comfortable with the Indians, often settling among them. They established trade relationships and supplied the natives with guns, which the Spanish were trying to keep from them.

Spain was the primary European power in Texas for almost 300 years. Its attitude toward the Indians was often inconsistent, changing under pressure from other Europeans. The monarchy in Madrid viewed this new possession as land to be secured against French encroachment and tried to use Indians as pawns in a power struggle. However, the Indians were practical and often took advantage of the ongoing strife for their own gain. Since tribes were separate and autonomous and held different attitudes toward outsiders, Spanish administrators attempted several methods to control native populations. Missions had proven successful in New Mexico, so several were established in the new territory. However, except for a few missions in the San Antonio and El Paso areas, the effort was a failure. Most Indians had no desire to give up their independence and traditions. The Spaniards fought continuously with several tribes while trying to maintain peace with others, in order to quell Indian resistance and halt French expansion. In the 18th century the Spaniards wanted to sustain peace with the Comanches, in order to discourage the Indians' devastating raids on their settlements in New Mexico and also to encourage the Comanches' hatred of the Apaches. The Spaniards could not control the Apaches and hoped that the Comanches would be able to destroy them. In the 19th century a similar technique was employed by the colonial governor of Coahuila. He persuaded several bands of Kickapoos, along with some Shawnee, Delaware, and Cherokee Indians, to settle along the northern and northeastern borders of the territory, hoping that their presence would discourage Comanche and Kiowa raiding of Spanish settlements and be a barrier to American expansion, which was becoming a problem.

In spite of Spanish efforts during three centuries of occupation to control and "civilize" the natives, the land which would become Texas remained largely unsettled and had less than 10,000 immigrants.

However, the year 1821 marked the beginning of profound change for resident Indians and of a new era in the history of Texas. Stephen Austin arrived in the territory with 300 families. They came not to colonize the Indians but to settle and work the land, to establish farms and homesteads and towns. While some of the Anglo-Americans were allies and friends of the Indians, others took the opposite view. Sam Houston had been a friend of the Cherokees in the East and was a strong ally while president of the Republic of Texas. On the other hand, his successor, Mirabeau Lamar, is perhaps best remembered for his comment, "The only good Indian is a dead Indian." As the conquering culture became dominant, the Indians either became "civilized" or were destroyed.

In an effort to contain the Indians, a reservation was established on the Brazos River in 1854. It was soon abolished, however, in response to pressure from citizens of the new state, and residents of reservations were removed to Indian Territory (Oklahoma). The next several decades were marked by continuous fighting and acts of cruelty by both Indians and Whites. The White man was fighting to claim the land. The Indian was fighting to save his world. However, it was the destruction of the buffalo, the lifeline of the Plains Indians, which ended 12,000 years of autonomous Indian societies.

COAHUILTECANS

Little is known about the origins of the Coahuiltecans. At European contact, there were more than 200 independent bands. They inhabited the dry, brushy country of South Texas and were one of the first groups to interact with the Spaniards. In the early 18th century large numbers of Coahuiltecans came and settled at the missions established for them. Soon European diseases and deadly attacks by Comanches and Apaches decimated the population. By 1800 most of the Coahuiltecan people had been destroyed or absorbed into Spanish society.

The environment of the Coahuiltecans was not a hospitable one. The winter could bring unexpected bitter cold, and the summers were hot and very dry. The land was rocky, covered with cactus and brush but few trees. Summers were sometimes periods of relative plenty, but in winter the people often lived on the edge of starvation. The Indians utilized every edible food, from the occasional buffalo to fish, birds, snakes, and insects. Deer, javelina, and small animals such as rabbits were never plentiful enough to provide the basis of the people's diet. They depended on vegetable foods for survival, including all kinds of nuts, seeds, and plants like cacti, mesquite beans, sotol, and agave.

Resources were scarce, and most foods were seasonal. There-

Interesting insight into some Indians' belief in a supreme being was illustrated in an excerpt from a book by Colonel Randolph Marcy. Colonel Marcy showed a Bible to a Comanche and asked him if his people had ever heard of it.

"He [the Indian] answered in the negative, and added that in his opinion this talk emanated from the God of the White man, as the Comanches' God was so far distant in the sky that they could not hear him speak, and when they wished to communicate with him they were obliged to do it through the medium of the sun, which they could see and hold converse with."

A Coahuiltecan carrying a burden

fore, small families were the basic social unit much of the year, and they usually moved every few days in search of food. During harvest season, bands composed of related kinsmen would come together to hunt, gather food, and visit. Bands moved within well-defined areas using natural resources. They regarded this territory as theirs and defended it against interlopers. However, there was no defined authority or law. Members of a band would recognize some man of outstanding ability as leader. His primary responsibility was to direct harvest activities. Bands were very flexible, and members could leave and join other groups freely.

All members of Coahuiltecan society were equal, and resources were shared. Other than a band headman, the only person seen as different was the shaman. If someone was adept at curing illness or wounds, he was recognized as a shaman, and he also conducted religious ceremonials. Supernatural beliefs were primarily an individual affair, but dances directed by shamans were sometimes held by one or more bands, usually in summer when food was plentiful. These were religious feasts and celebrations of good fortune. The dances lasted all night, and eating peyote was part of the ritual. They also were an opportunity for visiting relatives and friends, for making new alliances, and often for matchmaking.

The Coahuiltecans had little use for excess goods. Their tools and weapons were simple, and their houses were easy to assemble—reed mats and hides were placed over bent saplings to form low, circular huts. The people wore few clothes—a loincloth, fiber sandals, and, in bad weather, a robe of rabbit skin, coyote hide, or any available animal skin. However, they, like people everywhere, enjoyed ornamentation and decorated their clothing elaborately with seeds. They also used tattoos liberally, both as ornaments and as symbols. They were a hardy people whose endurance greatly impressed the Europeans. It was said that a Coahuiltecan could chase a deer all day without fatigue. These Indians were well adapted to their environment and survived in a harsh, inhospitable land.

THE KARANKAWAS

A great debate exists regarding how the Karankawas lived and from whence they came. While some scholars believe that they were nomads, others are convinced that they lived in permanent towns on the coast, venturing inland only for occasional hunting trips. Most conventional sources align the Karankawa language with that of the Coahuiltecan, which would indicate a close relationship. Others think that the Karankawas were Indians of the plains who came south and settled on the Texas coast. Still other scholars, citing linguistic, cultural, and physical traits, argue that they were Carib Indians who came ashore, probably by accident, and took control of the coastal area around modern Corpus Christi.

In 1528 Álvar Núñez Cabeza de Vaca may have been the first European to encounter the Karankawas in the Galveston Bay area. Karankawa-European contacts were often dramatic ones since both Spanish and French ships landed in their territory. Early relations were friendly, but eventually the Indians became wary and hostile toward the foreigners. In response to French efforts to settle in the area, the Spanish attempted to establish several missions among the Karankawas. A few Indians responded, but most were contemptuous of such a life. By the end of the 18th century European diseases and warfare had nearly annihilated the tribe.

The coastal environment was hot and humid in summer and mild in winter. Winters were very dry, however, and supplies of drinkable water were often dangerously low. The country was one of grasslands and scattered wooded areas and was home to many species of animals including deer. The Karankawas did not practice agriculture; they were hunters, gatherers, and especially fishermen. They ate plants and animals and relied heavily on marine life—oysters, mussels, turtles, fish, and ducks. The Karankawas had more natural resources than their Coahuiltecan neighbors, but many foods were seasonal, and they regularly exploited inland resources.

The Karankawas were divided into four or five bands of 40 to 50 people each. Each band was independent, and members recognized an outstanding individual as leader. There may also have been another man who functioned as a leader in war and raiding.

Accounts mention two major deities in which the Karankawas believed, but little else is known about their religion. Like other Indian groups, they had shamans who were skilled in curing and magic and who conducted band ceremonials. Rituals were centered around their dances, which were feasts held for a variety of reasons, both religious and secular. The most important *mitotes* (rituals with dancing) involved drinking copious amounts of tea made from the yaupon shrub. These celebrations were also social events between bands, which provided opportunities for visiting, trading, and matchmaking. The Indians enjoyed games, including wrestling, target practice with knives and arrows, and several kinds of ball games.

Europeans were fascinated by the physical appearance of the Karankawas. The men were tall and muscular and went about naked except for pieces of cane which they wore through perforations in the lower lip and in the nipple of each breast. Women wore skirts of Spanish moss and deerskin, and both sexes practiced extensive body painting and tattooing. The people smeared their bodies with alligator grease as a mosquito repellent. Shelters, more windbreaks than houses, were made of woven mats stretched over the windward side of an oval framework of willow poles. Dugout canoes were used near the shore but were not sturdy enough for unprotected water or bad weather. The Indians made both baskets and pottery, which they decorated and coated on the interior with natural asphalt.

The Karankawas resisted Spanish attempts to "civilize" them and were formidable enemies until their disappearance in the early 1800's.

THE JUMANOS

Spanish explorers often passed through Jumano territory during the 16th and 17th centuries, yet less is known about this group of Indians than any in Texas. The historical Jumanos apparently were related to both the ancient Puebloan societies of the west and the indigenous hunting-gathering groups which had inhabited the valley of the Rio Grande. In the 17th century these Indians occupied as many as 15 villages, but by the early 18th century Jumano culture had completely disintegrated.

The Indians inhabited the southwestern borders of Texas, from the vicinity of El Paso along the Rio Grande Valley as far as Presidio. It was an arid region with large sections of desert where farming was nearly impossible without irrigation. The Indians settled in valleys or flood plains where natural moisture increased chances for good harvests. Long, narrow stretches of valley along the Rio Grande provided fertile soil for corn, beans, squash, and tobacco, while the dusty uplands were suitable for hunting and for gathering wild plants as food.

During the 17th century, under their chief, Juan Sabeata, the Jumanos traded across the plains with groups as diverse as the Caddos of East Texas and the Pueblos of northern New Mexico. Archaeological evidence suggests that they were involved in this sort of trade as early as A.D. 1200. Some authorities feel that the "Jumanos" were actually a group of nomadic traders who win-

Karankawa Indians, by Berlandier, 1838

Ancient farmers lived in small groups in the desert near today's El Paso. Archaeologists call these people the Jornada Mogollon (A.D. 1200-1400).

tered with the "Patarabueye," who were the permanent residents and farmers of the Rio Grande Valley. Each village, or pueblo, had a leader called the war chief. The Jumanos had a rich tradition of ritual and music as evidenced by the elaborate ceremonies with which early Spanish expeditions were greeted. Further speculation on Jumano society must be based on complex Puebloan cultures of New Mexico and Arizona.

Unlike the multistoried dwellings typical of the Pueblo Indians in New Mexico and Arizona, Jumano houses were single family units, square and flat-roofed, constructed of timbers, and plastered with mud or adobe. They stood alone, clustered in groups. The people dressed simply. Jumano men usually went about naked except for a buffalo-skin robe, and the women wore deerskin bodices and skirts. The Jumanos may have been a pioneer people who brought a Pueblo tradition into a marginal environment, combining native traits with those borrowed from indigenous people.

THE APACHES

The Apaches were Athapaskan speakers, an indication that their origins were in the far northwest — Canada and Alaska. Over the centuries, they migrated down through the high plains along the eastern edges of the Rocky Mountains and were present on the southern plains and in Texas by the 16th century. In the early 18th century there were several distinct bands of the Eastern Apaches in Texas. The Apaches were surrounded by enemies: the Spanish on the south, the Comanches on the north, and the Wichitas with French guns on the east. During the 19th century the constant pressure on all sides caused Apache bands to separate and scatter, adopting different lifestyles. The Kiowa-Apaches became closely allied with the Kiowa and were typical Plains Indians; the Jicarilla band fled into New Mexico and Arizona and took refuge with the Pueblos; and the Lipans were pushed further into West Texas and Mexico onto lands so barren that gardening was impossible. The Lipan Apaches also adopted the horse and became mounted buffalo hunters. Apache culture changed and then was destroyed over a 200-year period, ending in the middle of the 19th century.

The Apaches moved through several environments during their history in Texas. Before the onslaught of the Comanches they settled along streams and valleys on the plains during spring and summer and raised gardens of maize, beans, squash, and pumpkins. During the fall and winter they became nomadic, following and hunting many species of animals, including the buffalo, which was their main diet staple. The villages were easy targets for Comanche raiders, who attacked them continuously. As the Apaches moved further south, they depended on the Pueblos of New Mexico to furnish them with the garden produce they could no longer raise and became more dependent on native plants as food sources, one of the most important being the agave.

"The Indian Maid," a watercolor of an Apache girl by Richard Petri

The basic social unit of Apache society was the extended family, consisting of father, mother, children, married children and spouses, and perhaps grandparents. Several of these families formed a band, which settled in a village or moved within a territory to hunt. The most important man in a band was the leader, or chief. He was primarily an advisor and director of activities with little real authority except through persuasion. In later years bands also had war chiefs. Bands sometimes came together to form alliances for defense and for war and raiding.

Religious beliefs among the Apaches were similar to many Indian groups. They acknowledged a supreme power, but individuals could approach numerous deities and spirits in nature. The people were particularly afraid of ghosts or spirits of the dead, because they believed that the deceased wanted relatives to join them in the afterlife. Shamans were involved with curing and foretelling events, as well as

Two Tigua women, c. 1900

A Plains Indian in the late 19th century

appealing to the supernatural to influence weather and fortunes.

Clothing among the Apaches was typical of many groups. Men wore breechclouts, leggings, and moccasins, and in winter added buckskin shirts and robes. Women wore leggings, knee-length skirts, and high moccasins. In the 19th century women added blouses to their attire. After about 1750 the Apaches lived in buffalo-hide tipis.

THE TIGUAS

The Tigua Indians of Texas are a branch of the same Indians who still reside in their ancient home in New Mexico. During the Pueblo Revolt in 1680 a segment of the group was with the Spanish when they fled to El Paso. The Tiguas established the village of Ysleta del Sur, where they still live. From the time of their settlement in Texas until the last fight with the Apaches in 1881, Tiguas served as scouts for the U.S. Cavalry and the Texas Rangers. (It was not until April 1968 that they received official recognition for their service by the United States Government.) In 1881 the Tiguas lived much like the Mexicans of the area, but the Indians are very conservative and have kept or revived many cultural traditions of Pueblo days.

The environment of the Tiguas was arid, but the land along the Rio Grande was irrigated and provided fertile soil for crops and gardens. When weather permitted, dry farming was practiced away from the river. In the 17th century Tiguas raised wheat, corn, squash, beans, and many other vegetables. They also had grapevines and extensive fruit orchards. They fished and hunted buffalo, antelope, and deer.

The Tiguas had an organized form of government. The chief held the title for life and was responsible for keeping tribal traditions and calling elections. The basic units of society were clans of maternally related kinsmen, who helped and supported each other in all activities.

The religion of these Indians has always been complex and rich in ceremony and tradition. Dances and celebrations were held throughout the year, commemorating both old traditions and Catholic feast days. Elaborate dances, chants, ceremonial paraphernalia and dress, and drums still remain part of the culture. The Tiguas also believed in shamans, some of whom were feared because of their evil power.

The Tiguas' culture is complex and very old. In 1540 they occupied four-story pueblos with ceremonial kivas, wore cotton clothing, and had highly developed pottery. Although their move to Texas modified many customs, they remain, even today, very conscious of their traditions.

THE TONKAWAS

The Tonkawas were first contacted in 1601 by the Oñate expedition north of Texas. By the 18th century they were found in the Red River area, and finally they settled in Central Texas. The Tonkawas were one of the groups displaced by the Apaches as they moved south across the plains. During the 18th century the population was decimated by disease and warfare, and remaining bands had consolidated into a tribe. This slowed the decline somewhat, but in 1855 the surviving Tonkawas were placed on the Brazos Reservation and later moved to Indian Territory (Oklahoma).

Central Texas was the Tonkawa homeland. To the south were the coastal plains; the Brazos bottoms were on the east. The Indians settled along streams and rivers, but they did not practice agriculture. Instead, they relied on hunting, gathering, and fishing for food.

Buffalo was the mainstay of their diet and provided material for clothing and housing. Tonkawas also hunted deer and rabbits and considered rattlesnake a delicacy. Fish and plants of all kinds—herbs, roots, fruit, seeds, and nuts—were important foods. The Tonkawas attempted gardening in the 18th century but were never successful.

Clans of maternally related kinsmen were the basic unit of Tonkawa society. These families lived and shared daily activities. Several small groups joined together to form a band, and each band was independent and autonomous from another. A band chief was the leader, and when the Tonkawas formed a tribe in later years, a tribal chief was also acknowledged. Shamans adept at curing were present among the Tonkawas, but little is known about any ceremonial roles they might have had. The people recognized several important gods but usually worshipped private spirits in their own way. A deep belief in spirits of the dead most directly affected their lives, and there were many taboos surrounding death. This could have been the reason for the ritual cannabalism practiced by the Tonkawas. Power from an enemy might be absorbed by consuming a bit of his flesh. On the other hand, desecrating part of an enemy's body through cannabalism might also destroy his soul, which was the ultimate victory.

The Tonkawas decorated themselves with body painting and tattooing. The men wore extremely long breechclouts, leggings, and moccasins, and the women wore short skin skirts. They lived in buffalo-hide tipis, but these were not like the typical tipi of the Plains Indians. The Tonkawas' were small,

A Tonkawa Indian, 1898

squat, and crude, and were replaced in the 19th century by flat-topped huts covered with brush, cloth, or skin. The Tonkawas were a peaceful people and were surrounded on all sides by powerful neighbors. In the 19th century they joined other neighboring groups, and the remnants of the Tonkawas were removed to Indian Territory.

THE ATAKAPANS

The Atakapans were not one tribe but a group of small related tribes. They lived in the southeastern part of Texas, an area largely bypassed by Europeans, and were never very well known. In the 16th century they shared some cultural traits with both the Caddos on their east and the coastal Karankawas. Some of the Atakapan tribes were attracted to Spanish missions in the middle of the 18th century, but the missions were abandoned, and the Indians later regarded the Spaniards with hostility. By 1830 most of the Atakapans had been absorbed into other tribes and the few survivors relocated to the Brazos Reservation in 1854.

Groups of Atakapans lived along the Trinity River near Beaumont and throughout the territory both inland and along the coast. The marshy, humid coastal region was unsuitable for agriculture while the inland soil was better, but the coastal area was rich in game, fish, and wild edible plants.

The Atakapans were primarily hunters and gatherers, utilizing deer, bear, and sometimes buffalo. Many wild plants were available, and the coastal people augmented their diets with fish, while the inland groups raised some crops, among them corn.

Like most Texas Indians, the Atakapans were organized in bands. There were at least four of these, and each had a headman, or chief. Each band was independent of the others. In winter, coastal families gathered in large groups and settled in inland villages to hunt buffalo. Some interior bands, on the other hand, lived in more or less permanent villages year-round.

The Atakapans believed in a creator and also that a prophet had laid down rules of conduct to their ancestors. Shamans were primarily curers and were regarded as special members of society.

The men's clothing consisted of simple breechclouts and moccasins with buffalo robes added in winter, while women wore skirts. Both men and women tattooed their bodies and smeared themselves with alligator grease to repel mosquitoes.

THE CADDOS

Texas derives its name from the Caddo word *tayshas,* which meant "friends." These Indians were some of the most fascinating to early explorers because their society was complex and had a government which Europeans could understand. They lived in vast East Texas forests, known now as the Piney Woods, where fertile alluvial soils produced crops which could be raised with little effort.

In the 16th century the Caddo Indians inhabited a large area of Louisiana and part of East Texas. There were actually more than two dozen towns loosely joined within three confederacies. The confederacies were the Hasinais, the Caddos, and the Natchitoches. For 200 years the Caddo region of Texas was the center of tension between Spain and France, then between Spain and the United States, and finally between Mexico and the United States. The Spanish established several missions in the territory in the 1700's, but the Indians were uninterested, and the effort was abandoned. By the 19th century the decline in population had been so rapid that Caddoan culture had virtually disappeared.

The Caddos were highly efficient farmers who harvested corn, squash, beans, sunflower seeds, and tobacco. They raised two varieties of corn with differing growing periods and at least five varieties of beans. They hunted with dogs and enhanced their diets with animals, fish, birds, and many varieties of plants, including nuts and wild fruits.

Caddo society was complex, and abundant food allowed the people to settle in towns of relatively dense populations. Large projects were shared, including planting, harvesting, and house building. The society was highly organized with a bureaucracy of offices and elected officials, each with specific duties. Positions of leadership combined both political and religious duties, and those at the top of the hierarchy—the *xinesí* and the *caddices,* or tribal chiefs—were hereditary positions. Unlike other Texas groups, some Caddos had full-time specialty jobs, such as the xinesí, some officers, and possibly some artisans. There is a great deal of evidence indicating that a few hundred years

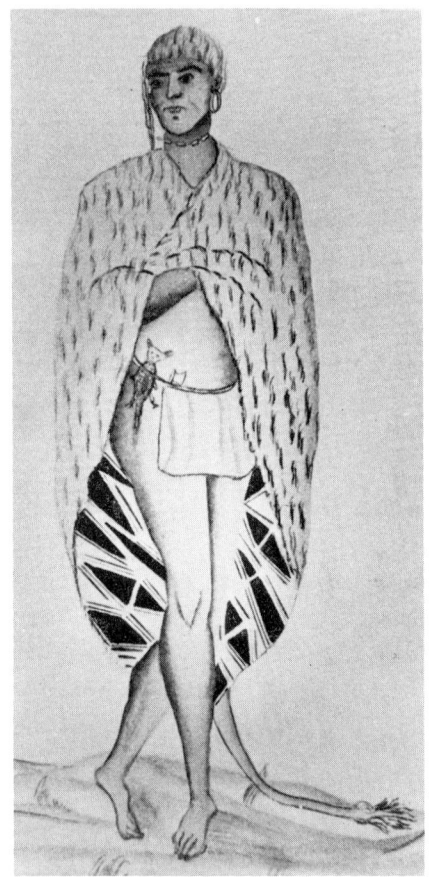

An Atakapa, by Berlandier, 1838

The Caddos of East Texas developed very large communities with expansive open areas and temples atop mounds.

before European contact, the Caddos were populous and powerful. At the George C. Davis site, now Caddoan Mounds State Historic Site, prehistoric Caddos lived in a large town or small city which included public plazas, temples, and burial mounds. Other such towns existed throughout East Texas, western Louisiana, southwestern Arkansas, and southeastern Oklahoma. Archaeologists have traced Caddo culture back as far as A.D. 700 and perhaps earlier. Theirs was a society which grew to dominance, flourished, and began to decline before the arrival of Europeans.

Religion was also highly organized, with temples and priests (the xinesí and caddices) to conduct elaborate ceremonies. The temple fire was kept burning at all times and was the source for all family fires. People believed in a supreme being, who rewarded good and punished evil, and a multitude of powerful spirits. Their many festivals and celebrations included the ritual cannibalism typical of most Texas groups.

The Caddos practiced cranial deformation and tattooing and used paint and materials such as feathers and shells to decorate themselves and their clothing. The deerskins from which they made their breechclouts, moccasins, leggings, and shirts were cured to an unusual black color. Caddo houses were large, often as much as 40 feet in diameter, and consisted of a circular framework of logs and poles, covered with coarse grass. The Caddos made baskets and mats but were particularly noted for their pottery.

The Caddo Fire Temple and Green Corn Ceremony

The most important religious place of the Caddo Indians was their fire temple. It was built much like their other round, beehive-like houses except that it was much larger. Their leader, the Gran Xinesí, maintained a perpetual fire fed by four large logs. The fire temples in East Texas in the 18th century were built on low mounds outside the villages. Near each fire temple was a small building with an altar, which only the Gran Xinesí and a few others could enter. Often several villages used the same temple. Inside the temple was the fire and a small square bench which held smoking pipes with feathers and pottery incense burners. Smaller, less important temples were constructed in the homes of the caddices in each village.

The most important Caddo ceremony was the "green corn," or harvest, ceremony which marked the beginning of harvest season in the year. Like all of the settled, agricultural societies of the southeastern United States, the time of harvesting corn and beans in the fall was when the people would know how rich — or poor — they would be during the next year.

Six days before the ceremony the men would gather at the house of a caddi where there was a small fire temple. Each day hunters went out for deer to collect skins to be worn during the ceremony. When all was ready, two older men at the large fire temple would rise and pray for more than an hour. Then, in turn, all of the caddices would eat, drink, and smoke tobacco. At midnight the assembled families would each place food offerings into large baskets. From then until dawn the ritual dancing and singing went on. The next three days were celebrations with dancing, feasting, foot races, and other contests.

THE WICHITAS

The Wichitas were related to the Caddos and resided near them in Texas. The Wichitas had migrated northward from around the lower Red River, but during the 17th and 18th centuries more powerful and

> *The Indians very generally smoked, and a few of them chewed tobacco. Their mode of smoking, however, was very different from that of the White people. I have no recollection of ever seeing an Indian fill his pipe and smoke it all himself. If he wanted a little smoke alone, he would roll some tobacco in a leaf, or small piece of paper, and smoke it. They smoked, with rare exceptions, in companies. . . . I let them smoke in my office. A half dozen or less would leave their seats and sit in a circle on the floor, and then the one who was to light the pipe would prepare his medicine by taking off a moccasin, or putting a smooth stone, which he carried with him, in the palm of his hand, and resting the bowl of the pipe on it to fill and light, or do something else of like importance. Then gravely he would fill and light the pipe. The first full puff of smoke he would blow up for the Great Spirit, the Father, who gave them the tobacco seed and caused it to grow. The next puff he would blow to the floor for the mother, the earth, from whom the tobacco came. He then appropriated a puff or two for himself, and passed the pipe to the next one on the left. The pipe would go around the circle until exhausted, and then it was put away. I do not remember ever seeing it immediately relighted and smoked by the same company. It was not unusual for them to draw the smoke into their lungs and expel it through their nostrils. In that way they seemed to get the full benefit of it, without wasting so much as the White people do.*
>
> *They frequently mixed kinnikinic with their tobacco for smoking, which consisted of the leaves of sumac, which had turned red in the autumn. It gave quite a different odor to the smoke, and was more injurious to the lungs than pure tobacco. When they decided to go on the "war path," they would smoke "the war pipe." On another occasion they would smoke "the peace pipe," both being solemn occasions.*
>
> *Lawrie Tatum*
> *from* **Our Red Brothers**

unfriendly Indian groups forced the Wichitas to turn south, and they again settled in North Texas. Several hundred members of the tribe were moved to Indian Territory (Oklahoma) along with many Texas Indians in 1859.

The Wichitas were primarily farmers. Even after they adopted the horse and could more easily hunt buffalo, meat was only a supplement to their diets. They raised corn, beans, squash, melons, and plum trees. They actively traded with other Indians, Spaniards, and Frenchmen. During the 18th century they sold slaves to plantation owners in Louisiana.

The Wichitas lived in villages and towns with populations sometimes exceeding a thousand. After harvest in the fall, people left their homes and spent the winter hunting and living in tipis. The basic unit of the society was an extended matriarchal family. People reckoned kinship through their mother, and women owned the houses. Each town had a chief and subchief who were elected by the warriors, along with several other officials and lesser "servants." As pressures from out-

A Wichita village surrounded by fields, encountered by the Marcy expedition, 1852

siders increased and their numbers thinned, the Wichitas united as a single tribe for the first time.

Wichita religion was rich in ceremony and tradition. The people believed in many supernatural beings and powers, and divided them into sky and earth, male and female deities. The supreme being as creator was the most important, followed by Bright Shining Woman, goddess of fertility. In addition to the public ceremonies, the Wichitas also had private guardian spirits. Shamans had their own societies and were primarily healers but were also recognized as village officials and, as such, directed ceremonies.

The most fascinating aspect of Wichita appearance was their use of tattooing. More than any other Indian group, both men and women had extensive tattooing on their faces and bodies, sometimes covering skin surfaces almost completely. Like the Caddos, the Wichitas lived in grass houses composed of circular frameworks of logs and poles covered with coarse grass. In addition to their pottery and baskets, they were noted for their woodworking and fashioned many articles of wood.

THE COMANCHES

The Comanches were the foremost adversaries of the European settlers in Texas during the 19th century. Like the Europeans, the Comanches were relatively late immigrants to Texas, arriving in the 18th century. The Comanches were related to the Shoshones to the north, with origins in the Great Basin above the headwaters of the Arkansas River, probably in Wyoming. They moved southward and, on adopting the horse, moved out onto the plains, where they controlled a vast region for almost 150 years. There were approximately 12 bands at one time, several making their home in Texas west of the Cross Timbers between the headwaters of the Colorado and Brazos rivers. From there they

A Comanche camp, c. 1850

ranged thousands of miles, especially into New Mexico and Mexico, in search of horses, cattle, and captives.

The plains were often bitter cold in winter and sometimes very hot and dry in summer. However, the land was covered most of the year with grass, ideal both for the Spanish horses, which multiplied rapidly in the vast, open spaces, and for the bison, or buffalo, which roamed the region in great herds except during the hottest months.

Buffalo provided the Comanches with most of the basic necessities of life—food, shelter, and clothing, but the horse furnished them with great wealth and power. They not only owned more than three times as many horses as any other tribe, but they controlled the southern plains which were the primary breeding grounds of the wild mustangs. Even Comanche warfare was primarily concerned not with the common Plains Indian custom of counting coups for war honors but with the business of maintaining and increasing their great horse herds. They were, like Old World horse and camel nomads, a proud, fierce, and wealthy pastoral people.

They also hunted many other animals, including antelope, elk, bear, and deer. They did not practice agriculture but gathered wild fruits, nuts, berries, roots, and cactus. Typical of Plains Indians, the Comanches made great amounts of pemmican. This food item, which consisted of dried buffalo meat combined with fat and berries or nuts, could be stored for long periods and provided food during times of scarcity.

The Comanches were organized into bands, never into a single tribe. Leaders had no real authority. Members of a band recognized men of wisdom or bravery as peace chiefs or war chiefs, but these men retained positions of leadership only as long as they exercised their power wisely. Councils were composed of all men of the band, and all participated in decision making. Families camped together and could change band affiliation whenever they chose.

There were few group ceremonies or dances in Comanche religion. The Sun Dance, which was a hallmark of most Plains Indians, was not a part of Comanche society. It was held only once in 1874 in a vain attempt to save the culture. The Vision Quest was an individual search for power from private spirit guardians. Usually at puberty, young men, with the help of shamans, would undertake such a pursuit. Receiving power meant responsibility for observing certain taboos and making and caring for a private medicine bundle. The people also believed in the Great Spirit as creator and in the Sun, Moon, and Mother Earth. Shamans were primarily healers, although their power could be used for evil.

Comanches dressed in the same manner as most Texas natives: the men in breechclouts, leggings, moccasins, skin shirts, and buffalo robes; the women in buckskin dresses. They decorated themselves, their clothing, tipis, and even horses lavishly with paint. They had little use for belongings and had no tradition of pottery or basketry.

THE KIOWAS AND KIOWA-APACHES

The band of Apaches which joined the Kiowa Indians during the 19th century became known as the Kiowa-Apaches and part of the larger Kiowa society. The origins of the Kiowas are unknown. However, they emigrated from the Dakotas about 1780 and settled in the Wichita Mountains of Oklahoma. They were close allies of the Comanches during the 19th century—in 1790 the two groups formed an alliance which was never broken.

Comanche and Kiowa societies were very similar except for several areas in social and religious organization. The Kiowas, unlike the Comanches but typical of other Plains groups, had warrior societies present in their culture, even one for boys. The Kiowas also had a rich tribal tradition of supernatural ceremonies and beliefs. Tribal bundles called the Ten Grandmothers were cared for by a special shaman, or priest, and the Sun Dance was practiced, an elaborate celebration of tribal unity lasting for several days. The Kiowas also kept a tribal history, or calendar, painted on buffalo hide, and the society had many myths and legends concerning the story of the people.

THE VISION QUEST

The Vision Quest was an integral feature of several Plains Indian groups, including the Comanches. It was a very important and solemn undertaking usually attempted for the first time by boys at about 15 or 16 years of age. The experience was an attempt by a young Indian to seek a spirit guardian who would share supernatural power with him, power which could protect him and strengthen him through life. Before the youth left on his quest, the band shaman, or medicine man, would counsel and prepare him in the tradition of his people.

Clothed only in breechclout and moccasins, and carrying a buffalo robe, pipe, and tobacco, the young man would go out to a high place some distance from camp. He would spend four days and four nights in that place, fasting and thirsting, while he smoked and prayed for a vision or revelation from some spirit being. The vision or hallucination might be heralded by any natural phenomenon—a sudden wind, the cry of a bird, the howl of a wolf, the scream of an eagle, the sight of a buffalo or even a creature as small as a lizard. The guardian would then speak, teaching the recipient special songs and explaining the power to be shared, along with the incumbent responsibilities, procedures, and taboos associated with the maintenance of the particular power. The spirit guardian also directed the gathering of contents for the individual's personal medicine bag. The medicine bag or bundle consisted of a variety of items, including special herbs, grasses, small stones, or animal skin, and certain bird feathers, each of which had a special significance for the owner and his acquired power.

Sometimes the Vision Quest was nonproductive—no spirit guardian spoke during the four days and nights. There was no disgrace connected with this. When it happened, the young man might prolong the search for another day or two, but, more often, he would simply abandon the effort and seek another opportunity later, when he felt circumstances were more favorable. Although the first Vision Quest was sought at puberty, it was usually only the first of many. The search for power was made on many occasions—for success in war, hunting and raiding, revenge, curing, and even in mourning. Individuals could also share power, and, if the responsibility of a certain guardian's power became too onerous, the owner could respectfully relinquish it to the spirit being.

The Kiowa Calendar Histories

Today most knowledge of the past is passed on to the future in classrooms, through books, films, and video productions. Indians, like all preliterate societies, passed on knowledge through storytelling. The Greek Homer's famous works, for example, such as the *Iliad* and the *Odyssey,* were told many times before they were written down. The Kiowas kept track of time and the order of events by using calendars, which were great spirals or lines of pictographs, or painted pictures, on buffalo hide. Each pictograph would serve as a reminder to the storyteller of the event. A black bar, representing plants without leaves, indicated that the event occurred in the winter. Summer was marked by a medicine lodge, noting the most important seasonal event. In this way, the Kiowa storytellers could be sure that they had told of events completely and in the correct sequence.

In the summer of 1859 the Kiowas went as far north as Kansas to a place called "cedar bluff." There they held their annual Sun Dance. The dance that year was remembered as the "timber-clearing sun dance" since most of the trees there had been cut down. The Kiowas remembered that they had gone that far north because of the many buffalo in the area.

Kiowa Myths

Scientists believe that it took millions of years for the earth and humanity to become what they are today. Fundamentalist Christians believe that it took God seven days. Archaeologists talk of Indians coming into North America 12,000 or more years ago from Asia across what is now the Bering Strait. Kiowas, like many other Plains Indians, believe that a Great Flood wiped out everything, and only Grandmother Spider survived. She was light, as spiders are, and could float. When she and Snake Man emerged from their log, she began planting her garden. In her garden was maize, or corn. Thus began the next cycle of the world.

Once a little girl was lured out of her cradle by a porcupine, who led her up a tree into the land of the sky. The girl turned into a woman, and the porcupine into a man, the Sun. They married and had a child, the Sun-Boy "Tah'lee." She became lonely and tried to escape the Sun to rejoin her people with Tah'lee. The Sun saw their escape and killed

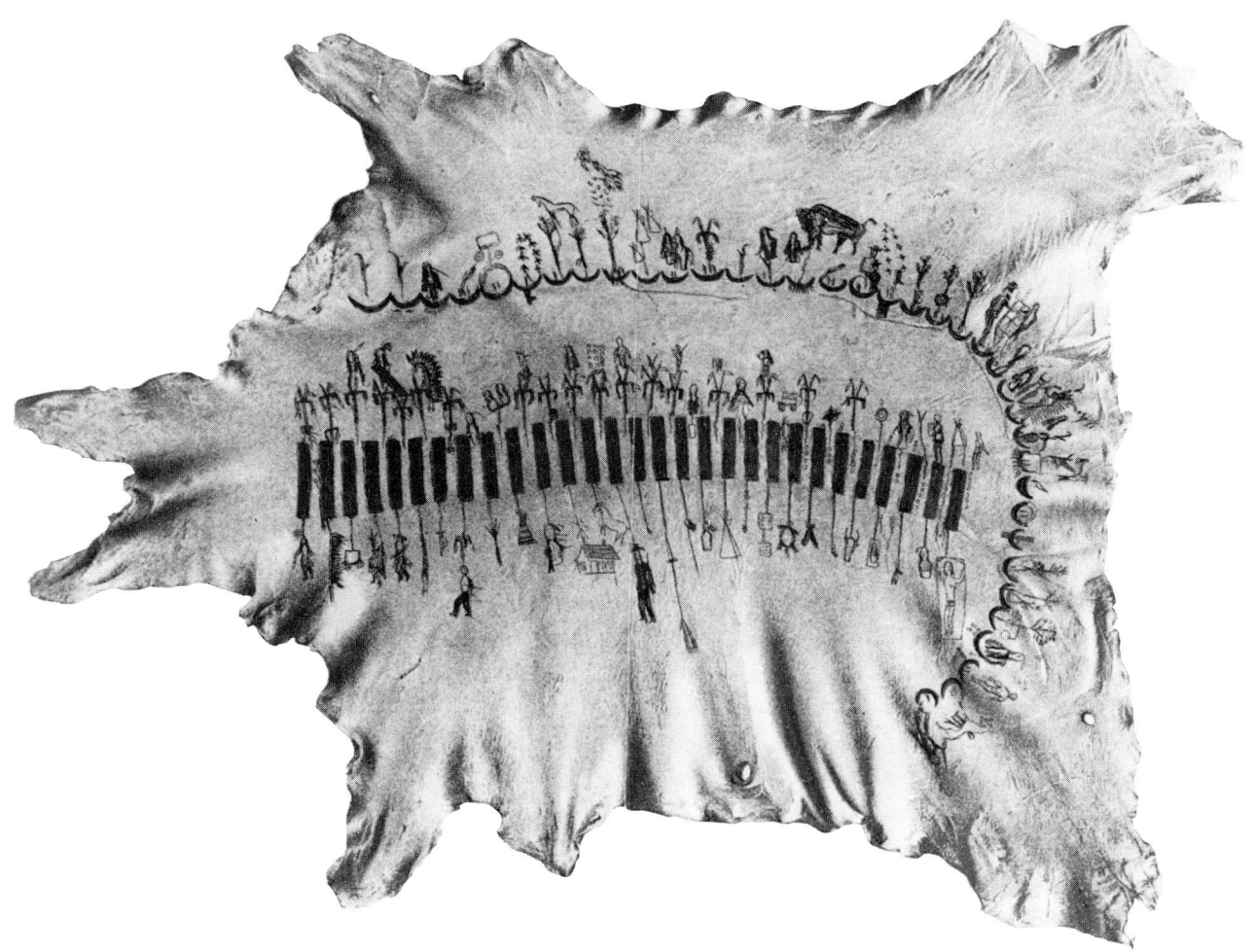

The Kiowa calendar kept by Anko

Late 18th century Texas Indians

her by throwing a wheel at her, but Tah'lee survived the fall to earth. He became friends with his Grandmother Spider. One day Tah'lee playfully threw the wheel which killed his mother into the air. It hit him in the head and split him into two half-boys, each with special powers. One half-boy disappeared forever into a lake, while the other remains today in ten parts as the spirit power of the ten Kiowa medicine bundles.

THE ALABAMAS AND THE COUSHATTAS

The Alabamas and the Coushattas are very closely related in language and custom. Their homeland was on the Alabama River, and they were members of the Creek Confederacy. In 1715 a group of the Alabamas migrated to the east bank of the Trinity River, while some of the Coushattas settled on the Red River near the Caddos. In 1787 some of the Indians moved to the Big Thicket, and by the early 19th century there were several villages in East Texas. The Alabama-Coushattas remained friendly with Texas after its independence from Mexico, and in 1854 the state purchased 1,280 acres of land for the Indians. The title was given to the tribe, tax-free

Two young Alabama-Coushatta girls, 1930's

and inalienable, and the surviving Alabama-Coushattas live there still.

When the Alabama and the Coushatta Indians came to East Texas, the Big Thicket was virtually unpopulated. It was a vast, almost jungle-like wilderness of thick vegetation. The region was teeming with life—animals, fish, birds—and an endless variety of edible plants grew in the virgin forests.

The Indians laid trails throughout the region and used these "traces" as well as water routes to obtain food. They hunted bear, wolves, deer, small animals, birds, and alligators, and had fishing camps on the lakes. Trade with Louisiana was also an important element in the lives of both societies.

Like other settled Indians, the Alabama-Coushattas had a well-organized system of social groupings. Families formed clans, and these came together in larger units called phratries and moities. These groups were present in each village, and members supported and aided each other in every aspect of life. Each town had a leader, the *micco*, who was chosen for his wisdom and oratorical ability, and he appointed a warrior chief to direct hostile activities. The position of micco was not hereditary but one of popular consent, and duties included presiding over tribal meetings and overseeing civil administration.

The Alabama-Coushattas believed that the Master of Life was the creator who breathed life into all people and animals. In addition, they believed in many good and bad spirits which were important in people's lives. Supernatural practices included many taboos but were also enriched with organized dances and ceremonies. Music played a major role in celebrations, and shamans acted both as religious leaders and as healers.

The Indians built rectangular-shaped houses of logs covered with thatch or bark. Clothing was fashioned from skin. The men wore long

THE VISIT TO THE SKY

In the beginning, four old men walked toward the west. They heard a sound—boom, boom. The sky opened, and they went up. One after another they ran through the sky.

"I am the panther, running through." Another said, "I am the wolf, running through." Another said, "I am the wildcat, running through." The last one said nothing, but he got caught and was killed. The others went on until they came to a place where an old woman lived by herself. There was a river nearby. The old woman told a boy to make a dipper and give it to these men. One after another they dipped up water and threw it in different directions. Then they crossed the river on dry ground.

They went a long way and found some people fighting, so they could not pass. The three men made cigarettes and smoked and blew the smoke all over the land. It became such a thick fog that the people could not see to fight, and the men passed through.

They came to a great many snakes piled up—about a mile of them. The men tied slippery elm bark all over their legs, and then they could walk among the snakes. Afterward they took off the slippery elm bark and threw it away.

They went on and on. At last they came to another old woman. They had eaten nothing and were hungry. The old woman cooked squashes and put three on each plate. As soon as a man had eaten these squashes, three more appeared on his plate.

The woman said, "You are dirty." She said, "Go fill a bucket with water and put it on the fire." When the water was boiling, she made them stand in a row with their backs to her, and she poured the boiling water on their backs and scrubbed them hard. They felt light after this and went on and on.

They went up on high to the Lord's place. The Lord asked, "Do you think you came a long way?" The Lord had a big telescope and said, "Come, look in here." They looked and saw their old home down below. The Lord said, "Do you want to go back?" They said, "Yes." The Lord gave them all kinds of seed—corn, sweet potato, and so forth, and made them sleep that night. In the morning they waked up in their old home and had the seed with them.

Alabama-Coushatta Myth

shirt-like garments, and the women's dresses resembled togas. In winter both sexes exchanged their traditional moccasins for some that were similar to soft boots.

THE KICKAPOOS

The Kickapoos were among the most conservative tribes in the United States. They were Algonquian speakers whose homeland was in Wisconsin or Illinois in 1672. They began moving slowly southward under pressure from the advancing Europeans. A Kickapoo band settled near St. Louis in Spanish Louisiana in 1765 but was on the move again after President Monroe forced the removal of Indians west of the Mississippi in 1817. By 1832 a number of bands were scattered from Kansas to Mexico, and one of these was a group of 300 which settled on the Sabine River near the Caddos and Alabama-Coushattas in Texas. The Kickapoos continued to resist Anglo-American encroachment and to engage in hostilities. In 1837 they were expelled from the Indian Confederacy and were invited by Mexico to form a settlement which would protect Saltillo from Apache raids.

Bands of Kickapoo raiders continued to enter Texas from Mexico and often rejoined their relatives in Oklahoma and Kansas. From 1851 to 1865 the Indians waged a war of vengeance against the Whites and continued to fight intermittently until the 1880's. They were, and still are, one of the most traditional of all Indians in this region of the United States, and they only returned to Texas to the Eagle Pass area in the 20th century.

The Kickapoos were a semi-settled people who resided in villages raising corn, beans, squash, and melons. After the harvest in the fall, entire families would leave their homes and spend the winter hunting deer, bear, and buffalo. Since their early history the Kickapoos had been active traders, both with other natives and with the European traders, and they often acted as middlemen between other tribes and White merchants.

Village populations varied from 50 to 300 people. Women were important in the society and built, as well as owned, the homes. Extended families were kin groups related through the maternal line. The village chief presided over the Council of Elders, which consisted of leaders of the main clans and their assistants. Leadership, however, was by influence rather than authority, and the leadership frequently changed.

Kickapoo religion includes supernatural "grandparents," which included fire, sun, and earth, and sacred tribal and clan bundles. The tribal calendar was full of celebrations filled with music and dances, but many aspects of religion also reflected fear. The Great Spirit had given the people a set of laws and offenses, and numerous taboos regarding food, houses, and sacred bundles had to be continuously observed. The supernatural beliefs of the Indians integrated all society, and man was obligated to deal with the spirits to keep life balanced.

By the time the Kickapoos arrived in Texas, many aspects of their clothing had been borrowed from Europeans. To their breechclouts, buckskin leggings, and moccasins, they had added calico print shirts, European-style vests, and hats, and were particularly fond of ribbons as ornamentation. The women had adopted flounced skirts and overblouses, and both sexes wore an abundance of jewelry. However, the people continued to live in their traditional houses. Wigwams were once covered with elm bark. In Texas and Mexico they were covered with cattail reeds. The Kickapoos were adept at basketry and also wove reed and cattail mats.

THE TEXAS CHEROKEES

Long before the "Trail of Tears" in 1838-1839 when most of the Cherokees were forced to leave their homeland in the southeastern United States, a group of these Indians had already settled in Texas. In 1794, during peace negotiations between the United States and the Cherokee nation, a subchief named Bowl and his band assaulted a flatboat on the Tennessee River and killed several Whites. Fearing retaliation, Bowl led the group down the Tennessee River to Arkansas and finally into Texas in 1819. The band settled on fertile lands between the Trinity and Sabine rivers in East Texas, in Caddo Indian territory, and formed an alliance with smaller groups of Alabamas, Coushattas, Kickapoos, Delawares, and Shawnees, who had been forced into Texas under pressure from European encroachment.

The Cherokees were anxious to establish homes and farms and remain at peace in a new land. In 1825 there was a short-lived attempt by a group of Cherokees and white settlers to establish a Republic of Fredonia, independent of Mexico, but it was unsuccessful, and soon the White settlers were looking covetously at the fertile lands of the Indians. Even Sam Houston, who had been a lifelong friend of the Cherokees, was unable to prevent them from becoming political pawns in the new Republic of Texas, and they were driven out in 1839.

The Cherokees were considered "civilized" by White standards because of their sophisticated towns and political organization. They had lived with Europeans for several centuries in the southeastern United States and had borrowed many ideas and customs, blending them into Cherokee culture. They were primarily farmers, and they hunted and fished to supplement their diet much as the White frontiersmen did. They built log cabins, cultivated various crops, including corn and cotton, and raised cattle, horses, and hogs. They owned gristmills and saltworks and wove their cotton into clothing for their families.

The Texas Cherokees maintained close ties with other Cherokees in the southeastern states and in Oklahoma. Texas Indians, like the rest of the Cherokee nation, became literate soon after Sequoyah, a West-

A Kickapoo family in Nacimiento, Coahuila, Mexico, c. 1900

ern Cherokee, developed a method of writing their language using English characters.

Nineteenth century Cherokee political organization reflected many American traits—the office of principal chief elected for four years, with three subchiefs, a council, and judges who presided over courts. Religion also had been exposed to years of European and American missionary influence, but it retained some ancient beliefs, such as the Great Buzzard who had created the valleys and mountains of the Allegheny for the Cherokees and the sun as author and giver of fire.

The Texas Cherokees followed the sad history of the entire Cherokee nation and, when driven out of Texas by President Mirabeau Lamar in 1838-1839, joined their fellow refugee tribesmen in Indian Territory (Oklahoma).

THE DELAWARES

When a group of Delaware families left their settlement in Cape Girardeau, Missouri, in 1815 and made their way into eastern Texas, they were continuing a migration which had begun over 150 years earlier in the Delaware Valley of New Jersey and Pennsylvania. Delaware Indians had been pushed westward and southward by pressures of European encroachment and had associated with many other tribes along the way, including the Shawnees, Nanticokes, Wyandots, Miamis, and Potawatomis. The Texas Delaware group probably contained 150 to 225 families, and they settled with other immigrant groups in Caddo Indian territory of East Texas. In 1854 they were moved with the remaining Shawnees, Wichitas, Caddos, and Tonkawas onto the Brazos reservation and were later removed to Indian Territory.

Over the years the Delawares had borrowed many traits—material and nonmaterial—from Europeans and other Indians, and had blended new ideas with old in Delaware society. When they arrived in Texas, they were, like the Cherokees, largely "civilized" by White standards, and their housing and clothing reflected years of European influence.

In spite of this, the Delawares retained their traditional organization. The tribal council still elected a war chief and a peace chief, and if a chief proved undesirable, the people could remove him through neglect; that is, they simply ignored him and followed another leader.

The major religious celebration of the Delawares was the Big House ceremony which lasted 12 days. The elaborate ritual incorporated singing, dancing, and feasting into a celebration of thanksgiving to the Creator for bestowing his blessings on men.

Delawares acted as scouts for the Army of the Republic of Texas against Comanche Indians, but in the end they fared no better than the Cherokees and also were removed to Indian Territory.

PLAINS LEADERS OF THE 19TH CENTURY

Only a few Indian names survive in Texas history—some because of their determined resistance to the White man's world, and a few because of their efforts to bridge the chasm between two cultures. Those Indians who lived or moved through the state during the 19th century and fought bitterly and courageously to preserve their freedom earned the respect of the military men who opposed them. Kiowas such as Satanta, Satank, Kicking Bird, Big Bow, and Lone Wolf, and Comanches such as Ten Bears, Horseback, Esa-Havey, Tabananica, and Quanah were among the last warriors to accept defeat and finally settle in Indian Territory.

Mow-a-way, a Comanche leader, was typical of Indians who finally realized the futility of resistance and gradually accepted a new way of life. He led a group on a raid into New Mexico in 1867 but was arrested and

Kicking Bird, a Kiowa chief and signer of the Medicine Lodge Treaty

Big Tree, a Kiowa chief

taken to Fort Leavenworth, Kansas. The following is an account of his journey as told to Indian agent and teacher Lawrie Tatum.

I supposed when we started that the soldiers were going to take us away off and then kill us. But we traveled on and on, day after day, in the wagons and were kindly treated. When one of the Indians was taken sick, I supposed that the White men would be glad for him to die. But instead of that they doctored him, and seemed to do all that they could to cure him. But he died, and then they did not throw him onto the grass for the wolves to eat, as I expected they would, but the commanding officer sent some of his men to dig a grave for him. They made a box and put him into it with all of his clothing, his bow and arrows; everything he owned they gave him. The hole that they dug was the nicest one that I ever saw. They made a little mound over him, smooth and nice. I could not understand why such mean people, as I thought the White people were, should be so kind to an Indian in sickness and after death.

When we had traveled many days we came to where there was a new kind of road that I had never heard of. There was a very large iron horse hitched to several houses on wheels. We were taken into one of them, which was the nicest house that I ever saw. There were seats on each side of it. As soon as we were seated the iron horse made a snort, and away it went, pulling the houses! Our ponies could not run so fast. It only [ran] a little while and then made a big snort and stopped at another White man's village. The iron horse kept running and snorting and stopping at the White men's, and the villages kept getting larger and larger. I had no idea that the White people had so many villages, and that there were so many White people. At length we reached Leavenworth, which was the largest of any of the villages. There the people were so numerous and the land so scarce they built one house on top of another, two or three houses [stories] high. These houses were divided into little houses [rooms] inside. The houses were built close together on both sides of the road. They were full of people, and the roads between the houses were full of people. I know not where they all came from but I saw them with my own eyes. I had no idea that there were so many people in existence.

After we were taken over one of the houses built on top of another, we were taken into a house down in the ground right under the other one. There was nobody living in it, but there were barrels of foolish water [whiskey] in it. There was some of it offered me to drink, but I saw that it made White men foolish who drank it, and I was afraid to take any, for fear I would get as foolish as they did. We were taken into a house that was built on the water [the Missouri River], and it could swim anywhere. It made no difference how deep the water was, it could swim.

There is where sugar comes from. I saw men rolling great big barrels of sugar out of the house on the water, and so many of them! Nobody need talk to me about sugar being scarce after seeing the large amount come out of that house that was swimming on the water.

A Comanche warrior in the late 19th century

After his experience, Mow-a-way, along with the majority of Plains Indians, became a part of society that White men in their haste to spread "civilization" tried to ignore. However, a handful of leaders emerged who tried to reconcile two cultures into a harmonious society.

One of the most famous Comanches during this period was Quanah, son of Peta Nocona, chief of the Quohada Band, and the White captive Cynthia Ann Parker. He was born in Texas about 1845 and became a major leader of the band after his father's death. His band refused to enter into the Medicine Lodge Treaty of 1867 by which the Comanche, Kiowa, Apache, Cheyenne, and Arapaho tribes were assigned to reservations. The Quohadas remained hostile and continued to raid and fight across the plains. In 1874 the Comanche medicine man, Isatai, urged Comanches, Kiowas, and Southern Cheyennes to attack buffalo hunters at Adobe Walls in the Texas Panhandle. He predicted that, if they did so, the White men would be driven out forever and the buffalo would return. A large force under Quanah's leadership launched the attack but suffered defeat, and their faith in their medicine was badly shaken. A month later Quanah and his band were involved in the disastrous defeat at Palo Duro Canyon, but still refused to accept the inevitable until June 1875 when they finally surrendered at Fort Sill, Indian Territory. During the rest of his life, Quanah displayed remarkable talent and insight in adapting to the White man's world while retaining many traditional Comanche beliefs. He had critics among the Indians, but his diligence in trying to work with the government on behalf of his people established him as a dedicated leader.

Placido

INDIAN SCOUTS

Several Indians distinguished themselves as allies and scouts in Texas military expeditions in the 19th century. Among these were Placido, a member of the Tonkawa tribe; Jim Shaw, a Delaware; and Showetat, a Caddo. Placido served the Texans between 1839 and 1862. He participated in many skirmishes and battles, especially against the Comanches. In 1862 a group of Indians representing several tribes attacked the Tonkawas, and Placido was among those killed. Jim Shaw, scout, interpreter, and diplomat, was a Delaware Indian who played an active role in establishing peace along the Texas frontier in the middle 1800's. He spoke several Indian languages in addition to English and

Chief Quanah Parker

served as an official representative in treaty negotiations for several governors, including Sam Houston. He helped bring about a treaty between German settlers and Comanches in 1847. In 1861 Showetat espoused the cause of the Confederacy. He raised and commanded a battalion of Indian scouts which served with the Confederate forces west of the Mississippi during the Civil War.

Mangus, an Apache chief

APACHE WAR LEADERS

Two great Apache war leaders, Victorio and Geronimo, gained a place in history because of their bitter resistance to reservation life. Both leaders led groups away from the San Carlos Reservation in New Mexico and waged guerrilla warfare through West Texas and Mexico, skillfully eluding military pursuers for several years. Victorio led his band from San Carlos in 1877 and remained free until his death in 1880 in Mexico. Geronimo, whose name became a war cry throughout the Southwest, left San Carlos in 1881. Although he was recaptured and returned to the reservation several times, he continued to escape. He rallied members of several Apache bands in the last major Indian resistance of 1881-1886. Following his final capture, he was sent to Florida in chains. In 1894 he was taken to Fort Sill, where he remained until his death in 1909 without ever being allowed to return to his homeland.

In the early 20th century, Geronimo wrote his autobiography and spoke about the Apache and the earth.

"We are vanishing from the earth, yet I cannot think we are useless or Usen (God) would not have created us. . . . For each tribe of men Usen created, He also made a home. In the land created for any particular tribe He placed whatever would be best for the welfare of that tribe.

"When Usen created the Apaches He also created their homes in the West. He gave them such grain, fruits, and game as they needed to eat. To restore their health when disease attacked them He taught them where to find these herbs, and how to prepare them for medicine. He gave them a pleasant climate, and all they needed for clothing and shelter was at hand. Thus it was in the beginning: the Apaches and their homes each created for the other by Usen himself. When they are taken from these homes they sicken and die. How long will it be until it is said there are no Apaches?"

CHIEF BOWLES

One of the most prominent Indians in Texas history was an immigrant to the state in 1820. The Bowl, or Chief Bowles, and his group of Cherokees were the first members of that tribe to settle in Texas. They came to establish homes and farms as permanent citizens of the fertile territory of East Texas. They wanted peace and title to their lands, and Chief Bowles spent a lifetime working on their behalf. He tried to establish Cherokee ownership through the Mexican government, traveling to Mexico City in 1823 in an attempt to settle the issue. When some of the Cherokees joined with White settlers in the Fredonian rebellion, Bowles refused to become involved because the Mexican agent promised the Cherokees land and fair treatment if they remained neutral, a promise which was unfulfilled. After years of broken promises the Indian leader remained hopeful and enlisted the help of his friend Sam Houston in his efforts. Bowles worked on behalf of the young republic as an emissary from Houston to the Plains tribes in an effort to pacify them and promote a peace treaty. A treaty was signed between the Cherokees and the provisional government of Texas, but it was

Chief Bowles

never ratified. Houston fought for the rights of the Indians, but public opinion was against all Indians, and his efforts failed. Bloodshed, accusations, and misunderstandings continued on both sides, and in 1839 the Cherokees were ordered out of Texas. Chief Bowles tried to play for time, whether to gather aid from other tribes or to organize his people for the trek was never known. However, his people headed northwest and were followed by Texas forces which engaged them in battle. On the second day Chief Bowles was killed wearing the bright silk vest, sash, and black military hat that Houston had given him and clutching the sword that was also a gift from his "friend and brother." Although Chief Bowles refused to aid Mexico in the Texans' fight for independence, and the Cherokees remained neutral, there was no place for them in the new republic.

The Indians of Texas Today

Through missionization, displacement, disease, and outright slaughter, few of the Indian groups which occupied Texas at the coming of the Europeans remain today. Today's Indians are generally recent immigrants to Texas themselves.

The Ysleta Mission church in El Paso which has served the Tiguas for over 300 years

THE ALABAMA-COUSHATTAS

The Alabama-Coushatta Indians still live on their reservation in southeast Texas. Although virtually all of the members of the tribes speak English and now attend public schools, most people speak either Alabama or Coushatta as well. The reservation is operated by the tribal council, and revenue from oil production, tourism, and government appropriations are dispersed by the tribe. No one owns land on the reservation; instead, individuals lease land, often for their lifetimes, from the tribe. In effect, this prevents sale of lands to nontribal members.

A major source of tribal income is the tourist center which has been established on the reservation. At the center Alabama-Coushattas perform dances and demonstrate traditional cooking and crafts for tourists. Much of what tourists see has been derived from the Indians' contact with other peoples. Many of the dances and costumes are borrowed from Plains Indians. Also, the "fry bread" is made of wheat, a European grain, rather than corn. The tribe is quite aware that the product being sold to tourists is not purely Alabama and Coushatta culture. At the same time, they live a way of life vastly different from the non-Indian society which surrounds them.

THE TIGUAS

The other reservation in Texas has been established for the Tiguas of El Paso. Urban dwellers for decades, the Tiguas retain their own culture within a culturally Hispanic community. Their tourist center is an attempt to recreate early Pueblo life in Texas. They are, however, fiercely proud of their heritage. In their tourist center one can find women painting pottery or cooking in con-

Fulton and Emmet Battise, Alabama-Coushatta chiefs in ceremonial clothing

temporary adobe ovens which originate far back in antiquity. Their restaurants and dances have also gained much attention. Aside from tourism, the Tiguas have formed tribal enterprises such as a dehydration plant for chilies and other vegetables to be sold to corporate giants like Del Monte.

THE KICKAPOOS

It has been said, with real justification, that the Kickapoo Indians are one of the most conservative Indian groups of North America. Since the Mexican government enticed them to settle in northern Mexico as a barrier to the raiding Apaches, their culture was virtually untouched by White or Mexican society until recently. Because a frontier fort officer wrote a letter allowing them to cross the U.S./Mexico border freely, they are considered citizens of both countries. In the 1940's some Kickapoos began to engage in migrant farm labor in the northern United States. Needing a convenient place to spend short periods, they constructed a cardboard house village on the U.S.

Señores Gonzales and Nanaté, Kickapoo leaders from Eagle Pass and Nacimiento

Kickapoos building a house

side of the international bridge at Eagle Pass. The houses were built much like 16th century wickiups which would have been found in their Wisconsin homeland. This location gave the Kickapoos easy access to the social services of the United States government as well as the convenience stores and fast-food restaurants of modern life. It also raised the ire of Eagle Pass citizens, who strove for years to remove the Kickapoos from their squatters' homes. In 1986 lands were acquired outside Eagle Pass for the Kickapoos, and an ordinance was passed banning construction in the Rio Grande floodplain in town. These two events have forced the Kickapoos to move, even though only about a third were initially willing to do so.

The Kickapoo homeland, however, is still in Nacimiento, Mexico, near a Black Seminole village. The Kickapoos live in Nacimiento much as they have lived for hundreds of years. The community has rarely been studied by anthropologists, and to this day, non-Kickapoos are not allowed into the community during the spring session of rituals.

THE BLACK SEMINOLES

Fleeing Black slaves joined the Seminole Indians in Florida to escape the plantation system. Eventually they were completely assimilated into Seminole society. However, as planters' efforts to recapture their slaves increased, the Black Seminoles fled Florida for Arkansas and Missouri. At about the same time the U.S. Cavalry was experiencing difficulties with their Apache scouts and so actively recruited the Black Seminoles. The cavalry was highly segregated at that time, and many Blacks were stationed at Fort Clark, now Brackettville. The fame of the Black Seminole scouts spread widely because of their skill and expertise. Today descendants of the scouts have been entirely integrated into the

Black society of Brackettville and the surrounding area.

THE URBAN INDIANS

In the 1960's the Bureau of Indian Affairs pursued an ill-fated and, most feel, ill-conceived program to integrate Indians from the Oklahoma, New Mexico, and Arizona reservations, among others, into the mainstream of society. The effort was based on the idea that America was a social "melting pot" and that all old cultures would be replaced by one "American" culture as the soup in the melting pot was stirred around. Both the idea and the program have been discarded.

During its existence, however, several thousand Indians, mainly Comanches, Apaches, Kiowas, and Navajos were moved to cities, given apartments and small sums of money and the opportunity to become part of the "melting pot." Today 25,000 to 30,000 Indians live in the Dallas-Ft. Worth area; several thousand more live in Houston and San Antonio. They are dedicated to keeping their cultural traditions while being employed in the same variety of ways as the other residents in those cities. Some of their organizations are designed to aid Indians with alcohol and drug abuse. Others exist to educate non-Indians about traditional Indian life.

In San Antonio in the past few years, a new group, the Native Americans Council of San Antonio, has been formed. Initially it had only a few members, but it now numbers nearly 100. Like other groups, these people strive to reinforce their own Indianness while educating the public about their culture. Even though they often wear suits and ties or blue jeans and work shirts, their lives are profoundly different from the non-Indians who surround them.

Attitudes about the role of traditional culture in modern life differ greatly among today's Indians. There are very conservative, traditional people living on reservations and in similar communities. Others are fully acculturated into non-Indian society. Most of those who work in cities and no longer live on reservations still feel very close to their reservation "home." They may often visit that home or plan to retire there someday. Often these people are more closely attached to the reservation than to Indians of other cultural backgrounds living in the same city.

On reservations throughout the country, liberal-minded leaders are attempting to operate tribal councils as cooperative businesses. Some reservations have vast mineral and tourism resources which bring money to the tribal councils. This money is spent on housing, education, and employment for the tribe. While this has good and positive aspects, it also expands the division between modern life and traditional values. Conservative members of tribes often disagree with this approach, desiring instead to retain the way of life, values, and world view of their parents. They also fear the loss of these traditions for their children.

Whether they live on or off reservations or are liberal or conservative, Indians today continue to reconcile traditional with modern life.

The 20th century Indians

FOR FURTHER READING

General

Hodge, Fredrick W. *Handbook of American Indians North of Mexico.* 1905; reprinted, Washington, D.C.: Smithsonian Institution, 1965.

Newcomb, W.W., Jr. *The Indians of Texas.* Austin: University of Texas Press, 1961.

Texas Before Columbus

Hester, Thomas R. *Digging into South Texas Prehistory.* San Antonio: Corona Press, 1980.

Shafer, Harry. *Ancient Texans.* Austin: Texas Monthly Press, 1986.

Turner, Sue, and Thomas R. Hester. *Guide to the Stone Artifacts of Texas.* Austin: Texas Monthly Press, 1985.

Bulletin of the Texas Archeological Society.

Relations with Europeans

John, Elizabeth A.H. *Storms Brewed in Other Men's Worlds.* College Station: Texas A&M University Press, 1975.

Coahuiltecans

Campbell, T.N. "Coahuiltecans and their Neighbors." *Handbook of North American Indians,* vol. 10. Ed. Alfonso Ortiz. Washington, D.C.: Smithsonian Institution, 1983.

Karankawas

Newcomb, W.W., Jr. "Karankawa." *Handbook of North American Indians,* vol. 5. Ed. Alfonso Ortiz. Washington, D.C.: Smithsonian Institution, 1983.

Jumanos

Kelley, J. Charles. *Jumano and Patarbueye: Relations at La Junta de los Rios.* Ann Arbor: Museum of Anthropology, University of Michigan, 1986.

Tiguas

Houser, Nicholas P. "Tigua Pueblo." *Handbook of North American Indians,* vol. 9. Washington, D.C.: Smithsonian Institution, 1979.

Wichitas

Newcomb, W.W., Jr. *The People Called Wichita.* Phoenix: Indian Tribal Series, 1976.

Comanches

Richardson, Rupert N. *The Comanche Barrier to South Plains Settlement.* Glendale, Calif.: Arthur H. Clark Co., 1933.

Wallace, Ernest, and E. Adamson Hoebel. *The Comanches: Lords of the Southern Plains.* Norman: University of Oklahoma Press, 1952.

Kiowas and Kiowa-Apaches

Boyd, Maurice. *Kiowa Voices.* 2 vols. Fort Worth: Texas Christian University Press, 1981.

Mayhall, Mildred P. *The Kiowas.* Norman: University of Oklahoma Press, 1962.

Mooney, James. *Calendar History of the Kiowa Indians.* 1898; reprinted, Washington, D.C.: Smithsonian Institution, 1979.

Kickapoos

Gibson, A.M. *The Kickapoos; Lords of the Middle Border.* Norman: University of Oklahoma Press, 1963.

Latorre, Felipe A., and Dolores L. Latorre. *The Mexican Kickapoo Indians.* Austin: University of Texas Press, 1976.

Ritzenthaler, Robert E., and Fredrick A. Peterson. *The Mexican Kickapoo Indians.* Westport, Conn.: Greenwood Press, 1970.

Cherokees

Clarke, Mary Whatley. *Chief Bowles and the Texas Cherokees.* Norman: University of Oklahoma Press, 1971.

Black Seminoles

Katz, William Loren. *The Black West.* Garden City, N.Y.: Anchor Press, 1971.

LEARNING ABOUT INDIANS IN TEXAS

Texas Indian Commission, Austin.

Reservations

Alabama-Coushatta Indian Reservation, Polk County. Visitors' center, demonstrations, gift shops, restaurant.

Tigua Indian Reservation, El Paso. Visitors' center, restaurant, demonstrations, gift shop.

Parks

Alibates Flint Quarries National Monument, Potter County. Where Indians for 10,000 years quarried stones for tools.

Caddoan Mounds State Historic Site, Cherokee County, near Alto. Remains of ancient Caddo town, museum.

Lubbock Lake Landmark, Lubbock County, north of Lubbock. Paleo-Indian site and interpretive center.

Seminole Canyon State Historic Site, Val Verde County, 9 miles west of Comstock. 6,000-year-old rock art, nature walks, museum, campgrounds.

Museums

Museum of Natural Science (Houston).
Panhandle-Plains Historical Museum (Canyon).
Texas Memorial Museum (Austin).
The Museum of Texas Tech University (Lubbock).
University Museum, The University of Texas at El Paso.
The University of Texas Institute of Texan Cultures at San Antonio.
Wilderness Park Museum (El Paso).
Witte Museum (San Antonio).

PHOTO CREDITS

Credits from left to right are separated by semicolons and from top to bottom by dashes.

Cover	Smithsonian Institution National Anthropological Archives, Washington, D.C.	Page 17	Edouard Charton, ed., *Le Tour du Monde* (Paris: Hachette et Cie, 1860), vol. 1
Page 3	Western History Collections, The University of Oklahoma at Norman	Page 19	Smithsonian Institution National Anthropological Archives, Washington, D.C.
Page 4	Corpus Christi Museum, Corpus Christi	Page 20	I.T.C. — I.T.C.
Page 5	New York Public Library, New York — Texas Memorial Museum, The University of Texas at Austin	Page 22	Allen Richards, San Antonio
		Page 23	Barker Texas History Center, The University of Texas at Austin
Page 6	Jim Zintgraff, San Antonio	Page 24	Barker Texas History Center, The University of Texas at Austin — Homer S. Thrall, *A Pictorial History of Texas, From the Earliest Visits of European Adventurers, to A.D. 1879* (St. Louis, Mo.: N.D. Thompson & Co., 1879)
Page 7	Office of the State Archeologist, Austin		
Page 9	Texas Memorial Museum, The University of Texas at Austin		
Page 10	The Thomas Gilcrease Institute of American History and Art, Tulsa, Oklahoma	Page 25	Western History Collections, The University of Oklahoma at Norman; Homer S. Thrall, *A Pictorial History of Texas, From the Earliest Visits of European Adventurers, to A.D. 1879* (St. Louis, Mo.: N.D. Thompson & Co., 1879)
Page 11	Artist George Nelson and I.T.C. — Mrs. Hunter P. Harris, Houston		
Page 12	Western History Collections, The University of Oklahoma at Norman; William P. Wright Jr., Abilene		
		Page 26	*Harper's Weekly,* April 17, 1886; Texas State Library, Austin
Page 13	Smithsonian Institution National Anthropological Archives, Washington, D.C.	Page 27	I.T.C. — I.T.C.
Page 14	Peabody Museum, Cambridge, Mass.	Page 28	Robert W. Parvin, Austin — Robert W. Parvin, Austin
Page 15	Artist George Nelson and I.T.C.	Back cover	Bill Wright, Abilene
Page 16	Smithsonian Institution National Anthropological Archives, Washington, D.C.		

QUOTATION SOURCES

Page 8	Randolph B. Marcy, *Exploration of the Red River of Louisiana* (Washington, D.C.: U.S. War Department, 1852).
Pages 16, 24	Lawrie Tatum, *Our Red Brothers and the Peace Policy of Ulysses S. Grant* (1899; reprint, Lincoln: University of Nebraska Press, 1970).
Page 21	Elma Heard, "Two Tales from the Alabamas," *Straight Texas,* ed. J. Frank Dobie. Publications of the Texas Folklore Society 13 (Austin: Texas Folklore Society, 1937).
Page 26	Geronimo, 1906 manuscript. *Geronimo's Story of His Life* (New York: Irvington Publishers, 1983).

INDEX

Italic numerals identify illustrations.

Agriculture 4, 6, 7, 8, 10, 11, *11,* 12, 13, 14, 16, 21, 22
Alabama Indians 20 *20,* 21, 27, *27*
Antelope Creek Focus people 7, *7*
Apache Indians 8, 11, *11,* 12, 26, *26*
    See also Kiowa and Kiowa-Apache Indians
Archaeology 5, 6, 7, *7*
Archaic Indians 6, *6*
Arrival in North America, Indian 4, *4,* 5
Art, Indian 6, *6*
Atakapan Indians 14, *14*
Austin, Stephen 8
Battise, Emmett *27*
Battise, Fulton *27*
Big Tree 23, *24*
Black Seminoles 28, 29
Bowles, Chief 26, *26,* 27
Buffalo, importance of 4, 5, *5,* 8, 13, 17
Caddo Indians 7, 14, 15, *15,* 25
Calendar, Kiowa 19, *19*
Cherokee Indians 8, 22, 23, 26, *26,* 27
Clothing, Indian *front cover, 3,* 5, 9, *9,* 10, *10,* 11, *11,* 12, *12,* 13, *13,* 14, *14,* 15, 17, 18, 20, 21, 22, *22,* 23, *24, 25, 26*
Coahuiltecan Indians 8, 9, *9*
Comanche Indians *3,* 8, 11, 17, *17,* 18, 23, *24,* 25
Contemporary Indians 27, 28, 29
Coushatta Indians 20, *20,* 21, 27, *27*
Delaware Indians 8, 23, 25
Esa-Havey 23
Fights-with-a-Feather *front cover*
Food 4, 7, 8, 9, 10, 13, 17, 22, 27, 28
    See also Agriculture; Hunting
Geronimo 26
Granillo, Trinidad *back cover*
Horseback 23
Horses, use of 4, 17
Housing, Indian 5, 6, 7, 9, 10, 11, 12, 13, 14, 15, *15,* 16, *16, 17,* 17, 20, 22, *22,* 28, *28*
Houston, Sam 8, 22, 27
Hunting 4, 5, *5,* 9, 10, 11, 13, 14, 17, 20, 21
Isatai 25
Jumano Indians 10, 11
Karankawa Indians 3, 9, 10, *10*
Kickapoo Indians 8, 21, 22, *22,* 28, *28*

Kicking Bird 23, *23*
Kiowa and Kiowa-Apache Indians 8, 18, 19, 23, *23, 24*
Lamar, Mirabeau 8, 23
Language, Indian 4, 9, 11, 21, 27
Lone Wolf 23
Mangus *26*
Medicine men
    See Shamans
Mogollon Indians 7, *11*
Mow-a-way 23, 24, 25
Mythology 19, 20, 21, 26
Native Americans Council of San Antonio 29
Neo-Indians 6, 7
Paleo-Indians 5, *5*
Parker, Quanah
    See Quanah
Patarabueye Indians 11
Placido 25, *25*
Plains Indians *12,* 23, 24, 25
    See also Kiowa, Comanche, and Apache Indians
Quanah 23, 25, *25*
Religion, Indian 4, 8, 9, 10, 11, 12, 13, 14, 15, 16, 17, 18, 20, 22, 23, 26, *27*
Reservations, Indian 8, 13, 14, 23, 26, 27, 29
Satank 23
Satanta 23
Scouts, Indian 12, 23, 25, 26, 28
Shamans 6, *6,* 9, 12, 13, 14, 17, 18
Shaw, Jim 25, 26
Shawnee Indians 8
Showetat 25, 26
Smoking 16
Social organization 4, 5, 8, 9, 10, 11, 12, 13, 14, 15, 16, 17, 18, 20, 21, 22, 23, 27, 29
Tabananica 23
Tattooing 9, 10, 13, 14, 15, 17
Ten Bears 23
Tigua Indians 12, *12,* 13, 27, *27,* 28
Tonkawa Indians 13, *13,* 14, 25, *25*
Trade 10, 11, 16, 20, 21
Victorio 26
Warfare, with Europeans 7, 8, 9
Warfare, with settlers 8, 21, 23, 24, 25, 26, 27
Wichita Indians 7, 11, 15, 16, *16,* 17